ESSENTIAL RELATIONSHIP HABITS

Simple, Effective Practices For Couples to Increase Intimacy and Build A Stronger Connection

Joan Scott

TABLE OF CONTENTS

INTRODUCTION

What is the mystery to getting a long and cheerful relationship? It is not fantastic heartfelt signals. The stunt is laying out solid propensities and doing those easily overlooked details consistently, without fail.

Keeping a relationship blissful is a regular work, assuming you work at it, you will hit the nail on the head.

In our present day and age, the unavoidable issues remain, for what reason do connections fall apart? How might you prevail in your relationship? Or on the other hand prevail in ongoing connections?

Couples who are probably going to part have more regrettable collaborations that offset the positive ones. In this way, making the accomplices scrutinize one another, show no help of one another, and don't exhibit love or appreciation. Fruitful connections in an entire have a harmony among good and pessimistic sentiments and the elements of the equilibrium are which separate blissful couples from disappointed ones.

This shows that seeing someone implies recognizing that making your partner cheerful and assisting them with feeling adored, protected, appreciated, and regarded isn't consistently about you and how you get love. So rather than asking what you can escape being with your accomplice, shift your outlook to how you can contribute emphatically to their life as well as the other way around.

There are innumerable ways of offering your relationship the care and consideration it requires to be a long-lasting one, and to create deeper connections between you and your partner. The best part is that a ton of them don't need an enormous change in your every day plan or huge load of cash.

CHAPTER ONE

WHY RELATIONSHIPS FAIL

The initial half year of a relationship is awesome. There are blossoms, sweets and many emoticon filled texts that are speedily perused and reacted to. You separate in the evening and video talk a couple of hours after. You share your food, wipe every others mouths and stroll down the road with your hands in one another's back pocket. You are cheerful thus enamored with your buddy. You can't get enough of them.

After a year you've separated☐

Be that as it may, you got going so well. The relationship was great. You were so sweet and in adoration with one another in some way the energy actually blurred.

How You Start won☐t ever make any difference!!

 Most connections go from hot, weighty and energetic to "meh" in around year and a half. The sentiments individuals☐ partner with being enamored the butterflies and the yearning scatter during this time and two or three starts to contemplate whether they should continue with the relationship.

There are assortments of justifications for why connections don't go all the way. Allow us to analyze them.

Absence of Trust

Absence of Trust is one of the significant justifications for why connections fizzle.

It tends to be an annoying uncertainty of passionate unfaithfulness, absurd unbending nature to an actual issue, or something that simply doesn't have a right outlook on the circumstance.

Over the long haul, these annoying trust issues become further bringing about a relationship breakdown.

Egocentricity

Pride is the most terrible of the multitude of major disastrous elements that have the ability to break any sort of relationship.

It has the greatest ability to kill our twelve lettered, Relationship, with such ease.

As anyone might expect, Selfishness is the main justification for why close to 100% of connections bomb nowadays.

We as a whole have Inner selves. In any case, in the event that not made due, it can prompt a major fiasco, especially with your friends and family.

At the point when the self image assumes control over, you wind up getting things in your way. Thus, you will more often than not give need just to your own commitments and penances while overlooking the endeavors of your accomplice.

Continuously, be aware of the way that it takes two to assemble a relationship. Consequently, you can't be the main one to choose every single activity or plan of life.

Inner self makes lopsidedness in the relationship by making us disappear gradually yet certainly from our friends and family because of which it turns out to be exceedingly difficult to fix.

Similarity Issues

Similarity is a solid point of support to fabricate your relationship on a strong establishment.

A few couples are together yet not happy with one another which is because of the absence of similarity between them.

Regardless of how much ever they attempt to get along, they are not simply viable in light of the fact that they hold tight to shallow contrasts that don't make any difference a piece.

Contradiction can cause more disappointment than it's worth and can ultimately destroy down the relationship totally.

Unfortunate Correspondence

Communication can either represent the moment of truth a relationship.

Unfortunate correspondence frequently prompts clashes seeing someone bringing about separations. Subsequently, great communication is vital for a sound relationship.

The closer we are to somebody, the more effectively we are harmed and will quite often hurt the other also.

Being a couple, both of you ought to actually impart your sentiments, regardless of whether they are positive or negative.

The accomplishment of any relationship depends on one's capacity to impart well.

Clashes are normal in any relationship. However, the genuine article is the manner by which well we impart and resolve it at the earliest.

Outrage

Outrage is a characteristic and sound feeling that everybody acts out and feels now and again.

Notwithstanding, it can turn into an issue in the event that it is excessively outrageous, difficult to control, or keeps going excessively lengthy.

Extreme outrage is one of the genuine worries why connections flop these days specifically.

Outrage emerges when things don't go as arranged, when you've been abused or wrongly blamed, or when there is a misconception. Aside from this, even pressure, disappointment, and tension can likewise bring about outrage.

While it's entirely ordinary to feel irate, it turns into an issue when you express it such that hurts yourself or others.

Outrage, harms your own connections as well as the general nature of your life.

Absence of Time

Not investing sufficient quality energy with your accomplice is additionally one of the fundamental motivations behind why connections flop these days.

In this universe of the web and innovation, life has become so occupied.

With every one of the responsibilities like work, gatherings, family obligations, a typical individual scarcely sets aside opportunity for herself not to mention invest energy with her accomplice.

This absence of time prompts troubled connections making space for the separation.

Working is significant, however don't put your business/profession before your relationship.

Regardless of how bustling you are, consistently set aside a few minutes for your loved ones, or probably you might need to lose them for eternity.

The Reality...

Connections are not consistently rainbows and butterflies. There should be rains, tempests, and floods more often than not.

There are no such things as an ideal relationship.

It's the manner by which you acknowledge the defects that make it awesome.

CHAPTER TWO

ESSENTIAL RELATIONSHIP HABITS- WHAT THEY ARE AND HOW TO BUILD THEM

Focus On Your Relationship

Focusing on your partner doesn't imply that you enjoy the entire day with them and leave all the other things behind. It doesn't imply that you ought not invest energy with your companions or have your own life. Focusing on your accomplice and why it's significant ought to be at the first spot on your list to have a durable solid relationship.

It is critical to ensure that you are focusing on your partner at each stage in life since it can likewise improve your relationship and prosperity. Couples have a lot of reasons with regards to focusing on their partner. Be it their work, youngsters, or different reasons that come out as comfortable.

What focusing on your partner fundamentally implies is that you ensure that you discover a few different ways to reconnect with your partner consistently. Whenever you invest in some opportunity to spend, only you two, it can prompt a more profound, seriously satisfying association.

There are a lot of motivations behind why focusing on your accomplice is a significant piece of a decent relationship. The main explanation is that not focusing on your accomplice or companion is certainly an elusive incline to not having that relationship keep going long by any stretch of the imagination. On the off chance that we pick our kids, work, or some other obligations and put the relationship in the secondary lounge, what happens when those obligations end?

Indeed, there are a ton of things in life that require our consideration and are significant, yet you need to try to recall that marriage and connections are intended to keep going for a lifetime. There will come when your children have grown up. The heap of your work will move away, or you resign. Your companions will have their own families to provide food as well. Eventually, it will be simply you and your accomplice. Try not to let the wide range of various obligations and interruptions eliminate you from the way that you promised to deal with everything alongside your accomplice.

For instance, great deals of couples truly do ascribe their ebbing love life to their kids. While kids are certainly a necessary need for guardians, you should in any case attempt to design around them. No one anticipates that you should remove a couple of excursion days from the children but instead figure out opportunity a couple of hours week by week to burn through alone along with your accomplice.

It is most certainly conceivable to set aside a few minutes for your accomplice, yet provided that you accept they are fundamentally important. It can assist you with beating a ton of difficulties and snags on the off chance that you have a strong establishment on which your relationship depends on. Assuming you keep on trusting that things will quiet down, you won't ever go anyplace on the grounds that things never truly quiet sufficiently down.

How would I focus on my partner?

A typical objection from couples is that their partner feels like they are not essential to the next. The actual relationship simply doesn't appear as though vital since the accomplice may continuously be shoved aside for youngsters, family, companions or even work. Once in a while, the experience could even feel new since a circumstance could emerge that makes them manage added responsibility or a wiped out parent.

Yet, anything the case it is by all accounts, quite possibly the most customary issue is that a few has likely fallen into an example. You both might be feeling disengaged and alone, yet the other individual may not know. This doesn't imply that you both might be contending and battling a ton, yet it doesn't appear to be going past fundamental casual banter or outlining strategies for the afternoon. You appear to remain stale with every day schedules and the equal lives where every one of you is essentially doing their own different thing.

In any case, the time has come to change this superfluous perspective. The most effective way to ponder connections is that you are both liable for keeping an eye on it. You ought to both be worried about focusing on your relationship and remain mindful of one another's requirements.

Learn the Ability to Understand On a Deeper Level

The ability to understand people on a deeper level is the mystery of enduring close connections, to a great extent since it makes us very mindful of the changes-enormous and little that are continually happening in ourselves as well as other people. By building your ability to appreciate anyone on a deeper level, you'll have the awareness that every one of us is continuously looking for in a better half. You'll naturally detect, through dynamic mindfulness and sympathy, the little changes in the elements of your sentiment that signal a requirement for activity.

We can possibly accomplish the sort of adoration we as a whole long for profound closeness, common thoughtfulness, genuine responsibility, deep caring-basically due to compassion, our inborn capacity to share passionate experience. However, to arrive at the tallness of sentiment we really want every one of the abilities of a high capacity to appreciate individuals on a profound level: sharp enthusiastic attention to abstain from confusing captivation or desire with enduring affection; acknowledgment to encounter feelings that could hurt a relationship whenever left to putrefy; and a watchful dynamic attention to assess us of what's working and what isn't.

We don't need to pick some unacceptable sweethearts, end up in different bombed relationships, or let the sentiment leak out of our relationship. We don't need to let clashing necessities and needs to interfere with two individuals who love one another. We don't need to surrender to weariness or quibbling in our affection lives.

We can possibly accomplish the sort of affection we as a whole long for profound closeness and common graciousness, genuine submitted, heartfelt caring-just due to sympathy and our inborn capacity to share enthusiastic experience. :

The ability to appreciate people at their core helps couples to:

- Effectively look for change in their relationship.

- View the difficulties they experience as any open doors rather than issues.

- Regard every one of the sentiments they have for one another.

- Keep the giggling in their adoration life.

- Focus on how they feel when their sweetheart isn't anywhere near.

Create Shared Ceremonies

Connections aren't just with regards to date evenings, end of the week escapes, and having intercourse. They can likewise have an otherworldly aspect that has to do with making an inward coexistence a culture rich with images and ceremonies and an appreciation for your jobs and objectives that interface you. It is then that you will start to get being important for the association you have become.

Probably the most ideal way to make shared significance is to discuss each other's fantasies, which are frequently profoundly associated with your pasts. One more method for making shared importance is to make customs and ceremonies for your coexistence as a team. Begin by conversing with one another with regards to the sorts of customs and ceremonies that you each had when you were growing up. What are your best and most exceedingly awful recollections? What might have improved them? How are these ceremonies for you today? What do they mean or represent to you? How might you like them to be presently? Share every one of your previous encounters with these practices and make exceptional ones of your own.

Finding what sorts of customs you two might want to present or go on in your relationship will help you in numerous ways: to feel the solace and trust that comes from depending on standard schedules, on turning towards one another, building more grounded bonds, and definitely developing your enthusiastic association. The more common significance you can find, the more profound, more extravagant, and seriously remunerating your relationship will be. These customs can include:

- Awakening each other.

- Breakfast, lunch, supper, or snacks together.

- Sleep time.

- Leaving each other.

- Rejoining.

- Sports/work out.

- Festivities.

- Dealing with one another when wiped out.

- Entertainment, games, play.

- Dates and heartfelt nights.

- Staring at the TV.

- Getting things done, tackling errands.

Whenever you examine the customs of association in your relationship, ensure that you and your accomplice both have the opportunity and energy for it. Recollect that this is intended to be a continuous cycle and not to be finished at the same time.

Regardless of relationship we're discussing be it companionship, familial, or heartfelt weakness is critical to encouraging a nearer, more profound, and more real bond with someone else. It keeps us legitimate with one another and ourselves, separates dividers, takes out the potential for miscommunication and misconceptions, and permits us to be entirely ourselves.

Practice Weakness

Weakness is the point at which an individual eagerly faces the challenge to uncover their feelings and shortcomings. This passionate receptiveness is fundamental in all solid connections, as it prepares for more profound agreement and brings out the compassion important for sound long haul relationships. With open correspondence, others can more readily connect with you and envision the subtlety of your sentiments.

It is totally normal to need to watch yourself and your feelings. Indeed, holding contemplations and sentiments to your chest and away from others is a type of insurance. Being excessively cut off to others-particularly in heartfelt connections or exceptionally dear kinships can misfire. The actual bond is less fulfilling, and your relationship might be significantly more defenseless to breaking. On the off chance that you don't permit yourself to be defenseless, your accomplice can't be anticipated to get what you want and need from them. They will without a doubt react in unsuitable ways. And afterward, in light of the fact that you don't feel upheld, you can dislike them and fault them rather than possessing your sentiments. And afterward, before you start to be powerless, you have a bunch to loosen up.

All connections are inclined to gaps; consider weakness the mortar that helps fill in the breaks.

In the same way as other things throughout everyday life, being defenseless doesn't constantly worked out easily. Truth be told, it very well may be truly hard to articulate our thoughts genuinely with another person out of dread of dismissal or judgment. Think about these means to building weakness:

- Talk about Weakness Itself.

- Name a Dread.

- Talk about a New Encounter.

- Share an Objective.

Practice Acknowledgment Of Your Accomplice

Acknowledgment is tied in with esteeming your partner's disparities. It's tied in with being adaptable, lenient and liberal. It's likewise about knowing how to think twice about, that we as a whole commit errors, and being prepared to pardon.

Acknowledgment doesn't mean continuously concurring with your accomplice - it's alright to settle on a truce.

However, it implies accepting that your accomplice is attempting to make the best decision.

Acknowledgment assists with keeping your relationship solid.

This is on the grounds that acknowledgment makes it more straightforward to see the value in the beneficial things about your accomplice and your relationship, driving you towards more prominent closeness and care for one another.

At the point when you and your accomplice feel acknowledged, you're more able to pay attention to and see each other's viewpoints and ideas. This can fortify your relationship, and it can likewise make it more straightforward for yourself as well as your accomplice to fill in as a nurturing group.

Every one of this implies acknowledgment makes a better, more joyful and more certain climate for the entire family. Bringing kids up in this sort of climate is great for their turn of events and can assist them with flourishing.

Acknowledgment can be fortified by:

- Investing energy in your relationship.

- Zeroing in on tackling issues.

- Being liberal with your contemplations.

Touch Regularly

Could it astound you to realize that there are medical advantages of clasping hands with your accomplice as you stroll down the road, or embracing when you get back toward the day's end? Or on the other hand setting your hand on his thigh or behind his neck when you're the traveler close to him in the vehicle? Do you realize it can encourage generally speaking health - for both of you - to approach out of the blue while she's tasting morning espresso at the kitchen table and your hands choose her shoulders or your arms encase her from behind? Same for sitting next to each other on the couch, legs against or crossing each other's, as you watch a film or an episode from your cherished series?

Contact can be a strong approach to imparting feelings non-verbally. It offers an inconspicuous and more nuanced approach in which we cooperate with others. Regardless of whether it is an embrace or a gesture of congratulations, contact can convey positive feelings like love and appreciation.

Contact or wavering in touch can likewise mean gloomy feelings. Envision a parent and youngster clasping hands when the parent firmly crushes their kid's hand. The present circumstance could caution the kid their guardian is encountering trepidation and sign an admonition. Wellbeing and association are fundamental for more close types of touch, like a long embrace. Individuals can regularly detect when somebody feels awkward or not responsive to that sort of touch. Contact likewise can possibly grow the profundity of correspondence when joined with discussion, eye to eye connection, and non-verbal communication.

Research proof lets us know that the presence of closeness in our lives - feeling comprehended, acknowledged and really focused on - firmly impacts our generally speaking physical and enthusiastic well-being.1 Closeness works from many sources, including the nature of an accomplice's responsiveness during discussion, the presence of sympathy, thoughtful gestures and liberality, in addition to - and this is frequently disregarded - the continuous experience of actual touch.

Contact can emphatically communicate a feeling of being acknowledged and really focused on - the passionate advantages. Contact additionally gives physiological advantages. In one review, accomplices were found to have lower levels of cortisol, the pressure chemical, on days when they delighted in more significant levels of actual touch like hand holding or embracing. (Undeniable degrees of cortisol have been found to expand pulse and circulatory strain). Researchers accept that it's the good feelings coming from actual touch - feeling content, feeling loose, feeling alert - that lead straightforwardly to bring down cortisol levels.

Contact probably improves the prosperity in all connections, however might be particularly significant in long haul connections where sex has come to assume a lessened part. Actual contact of a non-sexual nature - the embraces and presses, the handholding, the irregular contacts - can be a viable pathway for keeping up with closeness, with its many advantages.

Useful Contentions

It could seem like the best relationships are the ones where they say, "We never battle." Or, that they, "Consistently get along and consistently concur." Yet these encounters are neither solid, nor sensible. You want to have struggle with your life partner, however in a way that doesn't annihilate your relationship.

Perhaps you stay away from struggle since you would rather avoid it. Or then again perhaps you don't have a good sense of reassurance enough to voice your sentiments or conclusions. Anything that the explanation might be, staying away from struggle makes you cover your sentiments, and stuff them down all things being equal. In the long run, what you've been stuffing down will reemerge as outrage, disdain, or incredibly gloomy feelings toward your life partner.

For this reason it's useful to have sound clash in your marriage.

Presently, this doesn't involve having horrendous clash with shouting, seething battles that can't help your relationship.

Rather, struggle where you're expressing your genuine thoughts (and perhaps dissenting) is sound. You can contradict your mate; nevertheless, have a positive, fruitful relationship amidst the conflict. It is important to;

- Rethink Your Assumptions.

- Understand Your Quarrel Might Be Over Something More profound.

- Recollect That You and Your Mate Are In the same boat!

Practice Undivided Attention

Undivided attention is an example of listening that keeps you drawn in with your discussion accomplice in a positive manner. It is the most common way of listening mindfully while another person talks, rewording and reflecting back the thing is said, and keeping judgment and guidance.

At the point when you practice undivided attention, you cause the other individual to feel appreciated and esteemed. It's a strong establishment for any fruitful discussion in any setting, regardless of whether at work, at home, or in friendly circumstances.

Undivided attention includes something beyond hearing somebody talk, it includes the accompanying:

-   Focus completely on the thing is being said

 Tune in with every one of your faculties and focus completely on the speaker. Set aside your telephone, disregard interruptions, abstain from wandering off in fantasy land, and shut down your inner discourse.

To show the individual you're genuinely turned in, check out them and be aware of nonverbal practices. Utilize open, harmless non-verbal communication. Try not to overlap your arms. Grin, incline in, and gesture at key crossroads. Intentionally control your looks, staying away from any that convey bad introductions. Visually connecting is particularly significant. By and large, plan to keep up with it for 60% to 70% of the time you burn through tuning in.

- Reflect What You Hear

Reword what the individual has said, rather than expressing off the cuff feedback or impressions. Sum up what you've heard. Reflecting what the individual has said assists them with feeling approved and comprehended.

- Keep Judgment

Stay unbiased and non-critical in your reactions so the individual has a solid sense of security enough to keep sharing their contemplations. Create the discussion a protected zone where the individual can believe they will not be disgraced, condemned, accused, or in any case adversely got.

- Pose Open-Finished Inquiries

Keep away from "yes or no inquiries". They regularly produce impasse replies. All things being equal, pose open-finished inquiries about the individual to show you are keen on them and to energize insightful, extensive reactions.

On the off chance that you might want to all the more likely comprehend something the individual has said, request explanation. Try not to zero in such a huge amount on unimportant subtleties that you miss the 10,000 foot view.

-   Show restraint

Try not to intrude on, fill times of quietness with discourse, finish the individual's sentences, or top the story. Pay attention to comprehend, not to react. That is, don't set up an answer while the other individual is as yet talking; the last thing they say could change the significance of what they've effectively said. Try not to change the subject suddenly; this conveys weariness and restlessness.

Undivided attention assists you with understanding an individual's perspective and react with empathy. Your capacity to listen effectively to an accomplice going through a troublesome time is an important ability. It assists hold you back from expressing impressions and arrangements when the other individual truly simply needs to with being heard.

Be Empathetic

The idea of empathy includes putting yourself from someone else's point of view, rather than simply in your own. Compassion is basic as far as our more extensive spot on the planet and how we cooperate with the individuals who are unique in relation to us, yet it is likewise unimaginably significant in our own homes.

We could not typically ponder rehearsing compassion in our home lives, however that is really where empathy should start. For instance, assuming that your accomplice gets back home from a drawn out day feeling sad and exhausted, you can put yourself from her perspective and see exactly the way in which depleted she might be. Having sympathy should lead you to working on something for your accomplice when she has this impression, for example, creating supper for her or taking care of the children so she can have some alone time. This is called humane activity, and it implies that you can "experience together" rather than finding fault or misconstruing your accomplice when she can't connect with you since she is so depleted.

It tends to be challenging to need to rehearse compassion in a relationship. All things considered, in most present day associations, the two individuals work, and assuming they have youngsters, childcare obligations are regularly shared.

So assuming that the two accomplices are working- - regardless of whether one works at home focusing on youngsters - for what reason should the two accomplices try to think about one another's viewpoint?

Here's the reason on the grounds that, having sympathy is regularly the initial move toward sympathetic activity.

Empathetic activity is key toward a solid, cherishing relationship. It implies that you can draw in sympathy and see your accomplice's viewpoint and afterward act in a sympathetic manner toward them.

It's extremely simple to consider just your own point of view and your own concerns and disregard those of others. We are normally disposed to pay special attention to number one, and that is totally fine! In any case, when our own necessities are met, it's essential that we consider the requirements of our companion or accomplice second.

These methods for creating sympathy and rehearsing empathetic activity can direct you as you work on seeing the world through your accomplice's eyes.

- Talk about your considerations and sentiments.

- Follow up.

- Try not to condemn or analyze difficulties.

- Practice compassion over outrage.

- Use Caring Activity.

Apologize Carefully

Disagreements is neither abnormal nor is it generally something terrible. It very well may be useful and assist you with figuring out through problems; however pride can regularly hinder a solid conversation. At the point when we transform a contention into a study of our accomplices we feel awful thereafter, however we don't constantly apologize on the grounds that we dread surrendering power in the relationship. In actuality, an expression of remorse is quite possibly the most remarkable approach to reconnect with your accomplice and look for pardoning.

An expression of remorse can have a significant effect. Clarifying you are upset for how you acted and clarifying how you felt is a significant instrument for keeping up a solid relationship.

A genuine and insightful expression of remorse is a significant message to our accomplices that we give it a second thought, and a random "Please accept my apologies," isn't sufficient. All conciliatory sentiments aren't made equivalent.

A Successful Statement of regret ought to incorporate; letting them know how you feel, conceding your mix-up and recognizing the adverse consequence, and attempting to make what is going on right. Investing energy to make repayments shows that you're statement of regret is authentic.

Express Outrage Valuably

Sooner or later in your relationship, you will become irate at your accomplice. Be that as it may, how might you communicate outrage in your relationship without accidentally driving your accomplice away? Subject matter authorities agree, there are a couple of key things to remember.

Outrage can be totally legitimized, and, surprisingly, important in some cases to bump a relationship into an all the more impressive spot, yet before you attempt to communicate that resentment, you will need to arrive at a position of force. Outrage can be "debilitating." Simply consider it. Whenever somebody is coming at you with irate allegations, the regular response is to protect yourself. From that point, it can grow into a battle you never needed to get into.

However, to stay away from the battle that typically goes with a statement of outrage, there is something vital to remember. Communicating your outrage isn't tied in with finding fault. It doesn't have anything to do with your accomplice, yet everything to do with you and how you're feeling. It's like let your accomplice know that you're feeling dismal or cheerful.

Assuming that we handle outrage in our connections by first assuming complete ownership for our responses, we can come to the opposite side of contention with considerably more closeness.

You ought to continuously feel open to communicating how you feel to your accomplice. In any case, since outrage can place the other individual on the guard, it's not the simplest feeling to communicate. So here's the most ideal way to do it without driving your accomplice away:

- Search internally to check whether what you□re Enduring Is truly outrage.

- Think about your degree of outrage prior to raising the issue.

- Tell your accomplice what you really want from them right now.

- Use "I" explanations.

- If you feel yourself getting truly warmed, have some
  time off.

- Allow your accomplice an opportunity to handle
  things without expecting much else out of them.

- In the event that your accomplice has anything to say,
  pay attention to them.

Enliven Your Sexual Coexistence

Assuming you've been hitched for in excess of a couple
of years, odds are you and your mate have fallen into an
everyday practice - from who makes a garbage run to
who gets the children from school. And keeping in mind
that getting into a notch can be something worth being
thankful for, with regards to your sexual coexistence, it's
ideal to focus on assortment.

Enlivening your sexual coexistence can work on your
relationship with your accomplice and result in a large
group of medical advantages.

Getting lively with your soul mate can likewise help your
mind-set. Sex discharges endorphins, your mind's "vibe
great" synthetic compounds. Also, the chemicals
delivered during sex might bring down melancholy and

tension levels and lift resistance, says Needle. Having standard intercourse with your accomplice can likewise further develop rest, upgrade life span, and safeguard mind work.

All in all, how might you brighten up your sexual coexistence? Begin with these straightforward procedures:

- Take a stab at new things.

Over the long haul, most couples take on a genuinely unsurprising sexual content. To switch things around, have a go at a new thing. Begin with something basic like an alternate position or adding a visually impaired overlap to move your tactile experience. You could likewise present sex toys, pretend, spruce up, or change the landscape.

- Make out like young people.

Toward the start of a relationship, couples appreciate profound, provocative kissing, and they contact each other in stirring ways. In any case, as a relationship develops, that affectionate conduct can assume a lower priority in relation to errands and everyday exercises. Channel your internal teen and kiss, embrace, and cuddle your accomplice as you did when you initially met.

Doing as such will assist with keeping your marriage physically alive.

- Plan heartfelt exercises

Getting some down time to enjoy with your accomplice is one of the most cherishing things you can accomplish for one another. Alternate selecting an action and you'll associate all the more enthusiastically with your accomplice.

- Share your dreams.

Dreams are underutilized by couples, yet it's essential to utilize your creative mind and offer your most suggestive longings with your accomplice. Assuming you're feeling timid, set the disposition by lighting a few candles, switching off gadgets, and playing heartfelt music. When you're both inclination loose and personal, open up to your accomplice.

- See a sex specialist.

Assuming that you're actually feeling trapped in a hopeless cycle? Think about seeing a confirmed sex specialist.

Treatment isn't really held for issues, it very well may be about instruction, development, and sexual turn of events.

Practice Perkiness

Could you say your relationship is stuck? Provided that this is true, not an issue. As per relationship specialists, there are a few seemingly insignificant details you can do to make your relationship more perky and dynamic, assuming that is something you're hoping to do.

As a matter of first importance, it's critical to realize that weariness in your relationship is totally normal. Since there's a break in the relationship doesn't mean the individual isn't the One. Each relationship has their occupied and exhausting stages. So assuming you're content with your accomplice and your relationship yet feel like things are getting a piece normal, here are a few methods for making it more perky and dynamic:

- Experiment for yourself.

- Start to lead the pack and plan something fun.

- Perceive that you have an issue and make an arrangement to change it.

- Pursue each other once more.

- Get hot in the kitchen together.

Unplug

Thus, you're seeing someone. You love it when he awakens you pleasantly in the first part of the day, yet you disdain him when he's not getting a Wi-Fi signal.

Gracious, you thought we were discussing your real soul mate?

The issue is that both of you are undermining each other with your cell phones. Regardless of whether you're simply scrutinizing Face book or examining Buzz Feed□s most recent rundown, you're investing your energy with the Web and not with the individual who you really, actually love. Luckily, there are simple methods for being more aware of your cell phone use so it doesn't impede or totally assume control over-your genuine human relationship.

- Set It Aside

The most straightforward method for staying away from your telephone's diverting signals and hums? Quietness it and slip it into your pocket. Without notices blasting, you'll be way less leaned to stop your date to see what's going on in the virtual world. This is smart for your working environment efficiency, as well, to return home prior and invest more energy with your accomplice.

- Accomplish Something Non-Advanced

Regardless of whether your telephones are away, you're not going to be locked in with your better half in the event that you're daydreaming while at the same time watching Netflix. We realize that is an optimal night out following a monotonous week at work, for instance, yet try to remove a from the-case date when you're refreshed and reloaded. Like that, you'll have no real option except to draw in with and appreciate each other's conversation. Awwww.

- Switch Off to Turn On

Alright, so perhaps life has kept you at home or inside, however you actually need to have an associated, non-web associated date. It'll be your responsibility to switch off all of your innovation together and track down something amusing to do at home. Perhaps you'll whip out an old prepackaged game or cook together or pour a couple of glasses of wine and simply talk. Indeed, we ensure you'll adore this training such a lot of that you'll need to do it one time per week.

- Utilize Your Hands for Something Different

Regardless of whether its clasping hands or nestling, there are so many things that you can do as opposed to tapping your thumbs on a touch screen. The force of touch is unbelievable, particularly seeing someone: It assumes a critical part in producing and improving affection. Along these lines, put your telephone down and interweave your fingers for a sweet little love fest.

Try not to Fill Each Hole with Tech

It's our intuition to go after our telephones in vacation or snapshots of quiet. Sadly, regardless of the amount you and your affection need to tell each other, you'll in any case have stops in your discussion. That is not a remotely good reason to go going after your telephone. All things being equal make it a highlight hold on through the interruption and delay until your discussion picks back up. In the event that you're on your telephone, you may be slowing down it further. Furthermore recollect, your proceeded with presence is tremendously valued and required in circumstances like these.

You didn't get into your relationship so you could die the hours together☐ on your telephones. You had an association with one more human and based on that association to make your relationship. In this way, you must develop your affection and guard it from each of the interruptions that come from advanced gadgets. As such, put down the telephone and give that person a kiss: it's an ideal opportunity to become hopelessly enamored with genuine once more.

CHAPTER THREE

CONCLUSION

For a great many people, becoming hopelessly enamored as a rule appears to simply occur. It's remaining in adoration or safeguarding that "becoming hopelessly enamored" experience-that requires responsibility and work. Given the results, however, it's certainly worth the work. A solid, secure heartfelt connection can fill in as a continuous wellspring of help and bliss in your life, through all sorts of challenges, fortifying all parts of your prosperity. By making strides now to save or revive your becoming hopelessly enamored insight, you can construct a significant relationship that keeps going in any event, for a lifetime.

Many couples become attentive in their relationship only when there are explicit, unavoidable issues to solve. When these problems are settled, they regularly switch their consideration back to their professions, kids, or different interests. In any case, close connections require progressing consideration and responsibility for adoration to thrive. However long the soundness of a close connection stays essential to you, it will require your consideration and exertion. What's more recognizing and fixing a little issue in your relationship presently can frequently assist with keeping it from developing into a lot bigger one down street.